First published in 2007 by Incentive Publishing

This edition published in 2008 by Speechmark Publishing Ltd,
70 Alston Drive, Bradwell Abbey, Milton Keynes MK13 9HG.
Tel: +44 (0) 1908 326944   Fax: +44 (0) 1908 326960
www.speechmark.net

Reprinted 2009, 2010

British Library Cataloguing in Publication Data
A catalogue record for this book is available from the British Library

002-5516/Printed in the United Kingdom by CMP (UK) Ltd.

ISBN 978 0 86388 722 2

CONTENTS

About the Authors — iv

Introduction — 1

Theme 1: Places — 13

Theme 2: Issues — 41

Theme 3: Occasions — 79

Theme 4: Personal Development — 99

ABOUT THE AUTHORS

Pip Wilson

Pip Wilson is a beautiful human person who became an adult when he was 40. His work has ranged from Urban Street Gangs, Hells Angels, Special Needs groupwork with humans with drug and alcohol issues and more. He is also a charity CEO housing 172 young people in need, with 150 staff and 200 volunteers. Pip has far more scars than certificates! He believes that vulnerability is a strength, not a weakness.

Pip is the author of several books and the famous 'Blob Tree Tools', which can open the hardest heart, and is able to open up most meaningful communication in all cultures and contexts.

He is currently employed by West London YMCA; he also works freelance conducting groupwork/training/facilitation in the corporate and voluntary sectors.

Pip yearns for the uncomfortable, unease, dissatisfaction and daily refreshes the irritation. He believes that there is no such thing as a difficult person - only difficult behaviour.

Ian Long

Ian Long is the illustrator who worked with Pip to create the Blob Tree in 1988 and has since imagined, designed and drawn hundreds more Blob scenarios. Ian currently works as a teacher and youth worker.

INTRODUCTION

What are the Blobs?

They are neither male nor female, young or old, slave nor free! They are open to interpretation. Each character could be you, your partner, your best friend or a personal enemy. What is true for you might be completely the opposite for someone else. Blobs are a way to discuss issues in a deep, meaningful way and yet they can be understood by adults and children alike. You might look at a sheet and say that you feel like one Blob today, but tomorrow be a completely different Blob. You might find that a friend sees you in a completely opposite way! You could use each Blob Picture in a groupwork situation to stimulate discussion about how a team feels about itself.

The secret of how to use the Blob pictures is in asking the questions wisely! Open each session with broad questions before coming to the deeper issues which lie behind each image. There is no magic technique which will enable you to become a superb Blobster – just practice! You will find that children, young people and adults warm to being visually stimulated and having the opportunity to discuss their ideas and feelings.

Mix the Blobs in with other creative activities. Think of them as an element of the group activities. They might be your key element, but they need to be wrapped up with ice-breakers or perhaps music. Blobs are one effective way to help a group speak to each other.

Let us know how you do with the Blobs by contacting the publisher. Once you get used to the way they work you can start to explore more questions and judge the pace to take it for your group.

Happy Blobbing!

NOTES

www. blobtree .com

© PIP WILSON + IAN LONG 2005

NOTES

BLOB TREE 2

© IAN LONG 2005

QUESTIONS AND THE BLOB PICTURES

"We become fully conscious only of what we are able to express to someone else."

Paul Tournier: The Meaning of Persons

Questions are a very powerful tool. Those who work with people in education, law, care and personal development receive training in how to use them. A question such as, 'What can I do to solve the problem of poverty?' challenged Bob Geldof to initiate 'Live Aid' and Bono to urge the G8 leaders to end international debt. Talking about our own thoughts and feelings enables us to understand where we are and where we need to change.

Can you think of a question which changed the direction of your life?

Making time to talk about our emotions has become part of the primary National Curriculum in 'circle time'. Counsellors are skilled in the art of both asking probing questions and listening to the spoken and unspoken responses so that they can ask further questions. Job interviews depend upon them and those who are skilled in how to answer them move on in their personal ambitions. Church ministers use them to provoke us to think about our personal beliefs. Lawyers are trained in asking pertinent questions which expose the motives which lie behind our actions and reveal what we do not want others to know about us. We all appreciate people who want to listen to our problems and ask us the questions that give us the space to talk.

Who asks you the best questions in your life?

The most famous people in history were skilled at asking questions: Freud used them to reveal the thoughts of his clients; Jesus used  them to expose the motives of the religious hypocrites; Newton used them to understand the design of the Universe; Mother Theresa used them to stir up the feelings of those who came to see her work with the world's poorest people; Martin Luther-King used them to challenge the racist attitudes of America.

When did a question give you the space to come to your own conclusion?

There are different types of questions ranging from very superficial ones (How you doing?) to deep and probing ones (What started you crying?). When you use the Blobs remember that we all like to be questioned in a sensitive way. Sometimes we want to talk and other times we like to listen. Start with general questions, and then enquire about your group members' opinions, before finally giving them the opportunity to reveal their innermost thoughts. This whole process can happen the first time you meet together or it can take years.

Are there aspects of your work which would be improved by asking more questions?

Whenever Ian leads a 'questions assembly' at his school he is aware that for the first few minutes people are not really listening to the answers he provides, but to the attitude behind what is being said. By the end of the twenty minutes he is being deluged with issues on children's hearts. Valuing everyone's response to the picture is essential. It enables others to discuss more freely. There are no right or wrong answers. The Blobs provide your group with a chance to talk about an issue, or themselves, using an image rather than a set of words. For some people it may be as simple as pointing at a picture to describe themselves, for others it will start a conversation full of stories.

NOTES

_____

_____

_____

_____

_____

_____

_____

_____

_____

_____

_____

_____

_____

_____

_____

_____

_____

_____

_____

_____

BLOB QUESTIONS
Add your own: these are just to start you off

___

Starting Points (general questions)
Which Blob is happy?

Which Blob is sad?

Find a Blob that interests you.

Which Blob is definitely female?

Which Blob is definitely male?

Which is a cool Blob?

Which is an old Blob?

Which Blob is lonely?

In-depth Questions (exploring opinions)
Which Blob is the most positive?

Which Blob is the most negative?

Which Blob cares the most?

Which Blob do you not understand?

Which Blob is the leader?

Which Blob is likely to be in trouble with the police?

Which Blob is working for the police?

Which Blob is rich?

Which Blob is most likely to be taking drugs?

Which Blob could die soon?

Feelings Questions (getting personal)
Which Blob do you feel like?

Which Blob would you like to be?

Which Blob could God be?

Which Blob could God not be?

Which Blob scares you? Why?

Which Blob reminds you of your mum?

Which Blob reminds you of your dad?

Which Blob is the friend you have always wanted?

Which Blob would you keep away from?

Which Blob annoys you the most? Why?

WAYS OF USING THE SHEETS

Give out a copy of the sheet or project a copy for all to see using a projector.

Ask the group to view and choose which Blob they feel like in a certain group. This could be the group present, or another group that they belong to.

Ask them to share their ideas in threes or fours (larger group sharing is good but can take longer).

Feedback to the whole group – a fellow member speaks on another's behalf.

Mail a copy so that each person in your group can think about the picture in advance.

Colour in the different answers to your questions so that you can see the different responses each person makes.

Enlarge one copy and ask each person to colour in/mark their character so that you can see how the whole group fits together.

Ask each person to predict where one person is on the sheet and why. Then that person can share their own response.

Ask each person to predict where all of their small group are on the sheet and share within their small group.

Identify where you are and where you would like to be and discuss how you could get there.

Give yourself time to think on your own about the questions before sharing the sheet with others. A teacher can only share what they have learned through experience.

THEME 1: PLACES
CONTENTS

Blob Beach 17

Blob Choir 19

Blob Church 21

Blob Cinema 23

Blob City 25

Blob Cliff 27

Blob Concert 29

Blob Disco 31

Blob Homes 33

Blob Playground 35

Blob Staffroom 37

Blob Village 39

THEME 1: PLACES

Places are good to introduce Blobs with as they are simply situations people experience. Almost everyone will have had some of the feelings in each place which will enable them to offer their thoughts. Each place has many interpretations so take the opportunity to explore what the scene conjures up or symbolises for each member of your group.

Blob Beach: There are people who enter the water and people who do not. What could this symbolise? There are issues of size and confidence going on within the picture.

NOTES

_____

_____

_____

_____

_____

_____

_____

_____

_____

_____

_____

_____

_____

_____

_____

_____

Blob Choir: Even if the group has no involvement with singing, take the time to explore the relationships within this image. How would you feel as the conductor?

NOTES

_____

_____

_____

_____

_____

_____

_____

_____

_____

_____

_____

_____

_____

_____

_____

Blob Church: Two billion people go to church each week in the world. How do you think they feel? Could you see ways to improve things?

NOTES

_____

_____

_____

_____

_____

_____

_____

_____

_____

_____

_____

_____

_____

_____

_____

_____

BLOB CHURCH

www.blobtree.com

© IAN LONG 2004
+ PIP WILSON

Blob Cinema: We love the intimacy and darkness of a clean cinema. Would you like to be there? Where would you sit? Who would you avoid?

NOTES

_____

_____

_____

_____

_____

_____

_____

_____

_____

_____

_____

_____

_____

_____

_____

_____

_____

Blob City: Remember the first time you went to the big city? This Blob has discovered fame. Describe his experience. Who would you talk to?

NOTES

_____

_____

_____

_____

_____

_____

_____

_____

_____

_____

_____

_____

_____

_____

_____

Blob Cliff: A cliff is a dangerous place at the best of times. Why are people falling off? Who is trying to stop them? What does this symbolise?

NOTES

_____

_____

_____

_____

_____

_____

_____

_____

_____

_____

_____

_____

_____

_____

_____

_____

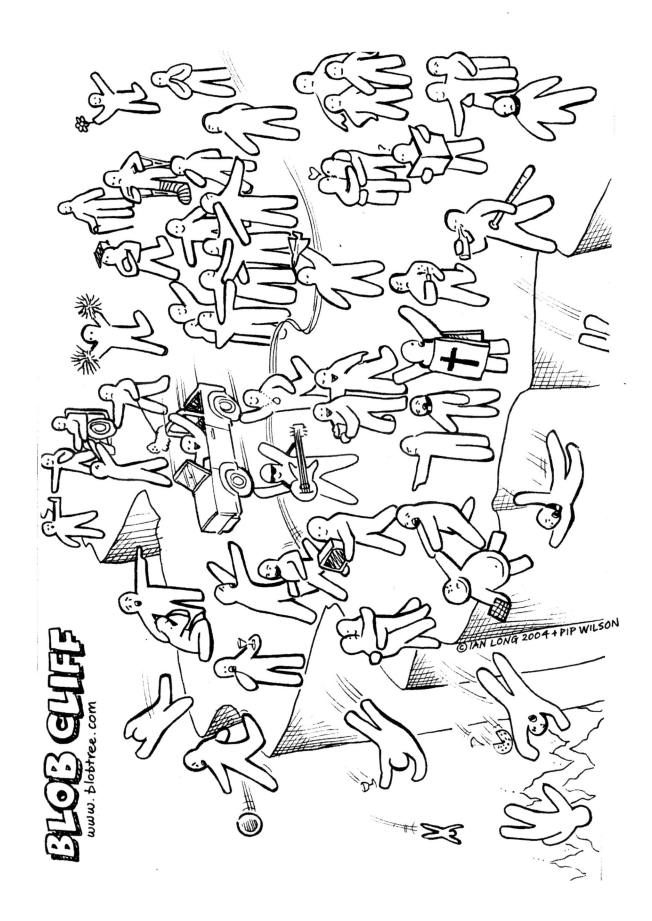

BLOB CLIFF
www.blobtree.com

Blob Concert: This concert is poorly attended but the feelings are clear. What job would you like there? Are you in the audience or on the stage?

NOTES

_____

_____

_____

_____

_____

_____

_____

_____

_____

_____

_____

_____

_____

_____

_____

_____

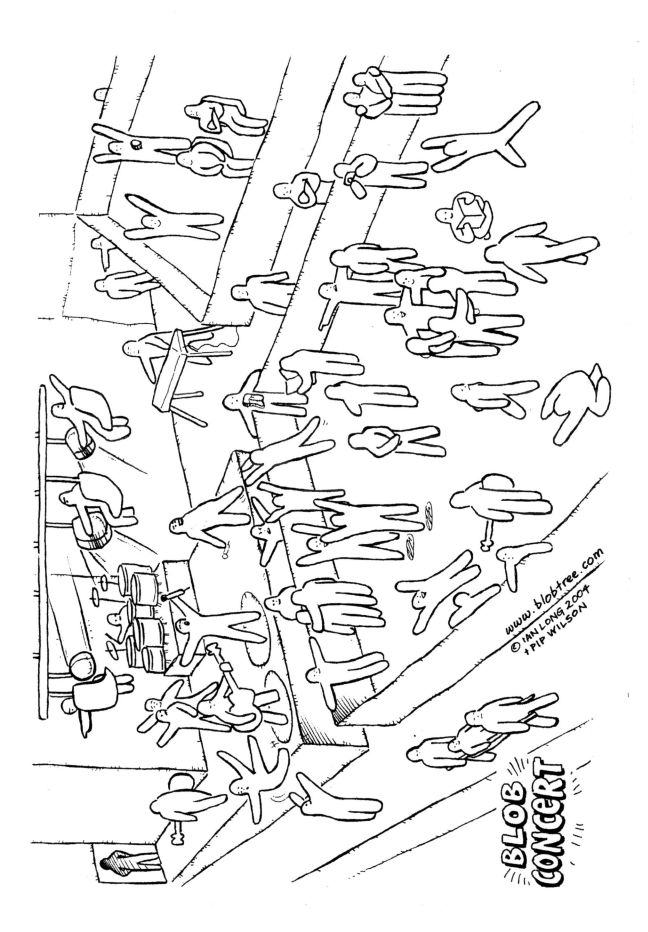

BLOB CONCERT

www.blobtree.com
© IAN LONG 2004
‡ PIP WILSON

Blob Disco: The school lights go off and it is your chance to talk to the Blob of your dreams. Do you make it? What happens next? Do you like to dance?

NOTES

_____

_____

_____

_____

_____

_____

_____

_____

_____

_____

_____

_____

_____

_____

_____

_____

BLOB DISCO

Blob Homes: Big issues of poverty and wealth clash on the page. Could you live everywhere?

NOTES

_____

_____

_____

_____

_____

_____

_____

_____

_____

_____

_____

_____

_____

_____

_____

_____

_____

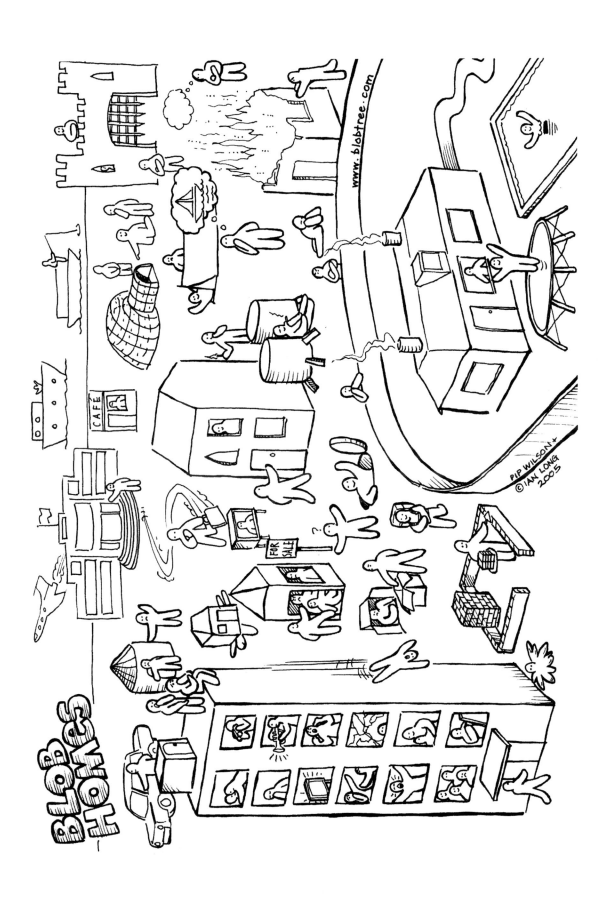

Blob Playground: Most children love to play. Most children find this their favourite part of school. Can you find the danger points? Who is being bullied?

NOTES

_____

_____

_____

_____

_____

_____

_____

_____

_____

_____

_____

_____

_____

_____

_____

_____

BLOB PLAYGROUND

www.blobtree.com

PIP WILSON +
©IAN LONG 2005

Blob Staffroom: Teachers can be like kids when the staffroom door is shut. Why are some of them hiding? Who is about to scream? Who do you avoid?

NOTES

_____

_____

_____

_____

_____

_____

_____

_____

_____

_____

_____

_____

_____

_____

_____

_____

_____

Blob Village: It is a small place but lots of issues walk the streets. Can you find a happy family? Where do you go? Where do you avoid? Who can you find to help?

NOTES

_____

_____

_____

_____

_____

_____

_____

_____

_____

_____

_____

_____

_____

_____

_____

_____

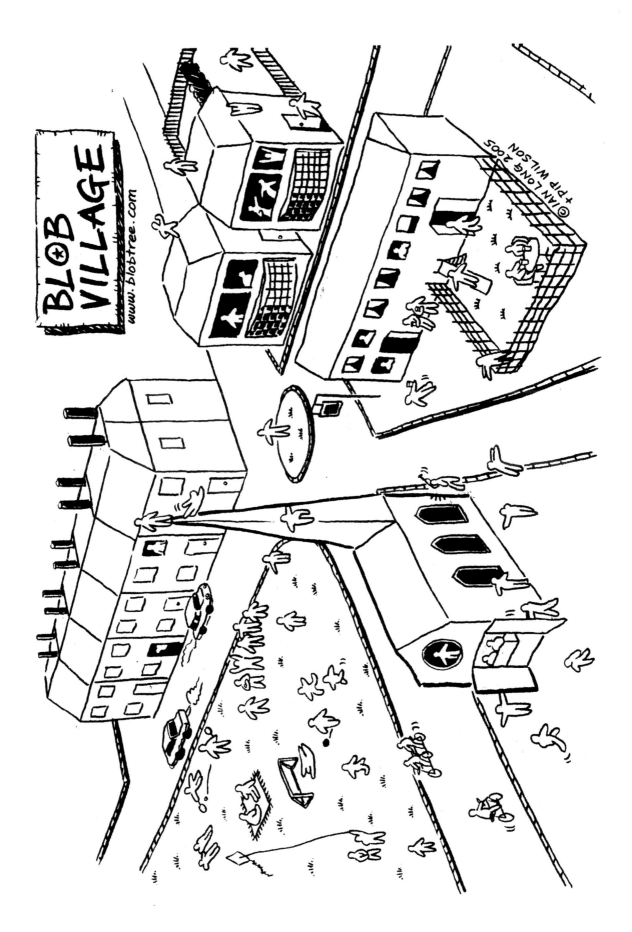

BLOB VILLAGE

www.blobtree.com

© IAN LONG 2005 + PIP WILSON

THEME 2: ISSUES

CONTENTS

Blob Bullying 45

Blob Death 47

Blob Disaster 49

Blob Divide 51

Blob Fame 53

Blob Families 55

Blob Feast 57

Blob Money 59

Blob Parents 61

Blob Protests 63

Blob Romance 65

Blob Sin 67

Blob Sleep 69

Blob Talk 71

Blob v Blob 73

Blob Water Safety 75

Blob World 77

THEME 2: ISSUES

Issues start to open up how people think and feel about lots of important areas of life. Being bullied can scar you for life. Families are wonderful, hellish or sometimes a mixture. Handle these images with care. The key to emphasise is that there is no right or wrong, only our own unique interpretation. No one needs to be threatened. Sharing our opinions helps us to hear what we think alongside what others think.

Blob Bullying: Bullying happens at all levels of society and yet people often cannot talk about it. Let group members explore/describe the different types. Which one have you experienced? Is bullying ever acceptable?

NOTES

_____

_____

_____

_____

_____

_____

_____

_____

_____

_____

_____

_____

_____

_____

_____

Blob Death: What we believe happens after death affects how we live. Which Blob values life? What is the best way to die? Where do we go?

NOTES

_____

_____

_____

_____

_____

_____

_____

_____

_____

_____

_____

_____

_____

_____

_____

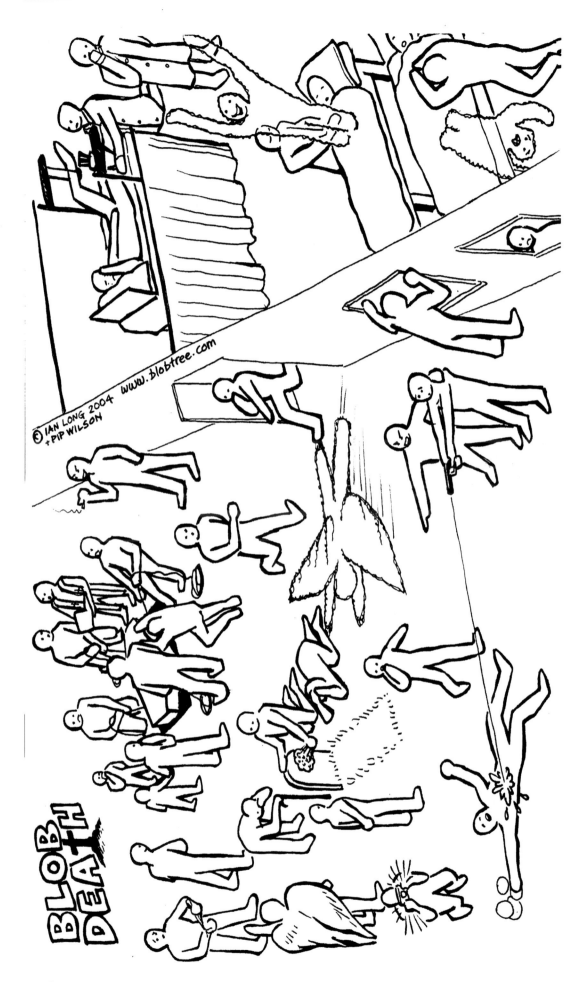

47

Blob Disaster: Earthquakes are terrible to live through. They are awful to watch from a distance. What could this symbolise? Which shock in your life has devastated you?

NOTES

_____

_____

_____

_____

_____

_____

_____

_____

_____

_____

_____

_____

_____

_____

_____

_____

_____

BLOB DISASTER
©IAN LONG 2005 + PIP WILSON

www.blobtree.com

Blob Divide: Tensions exist everywhere. Which Blob heals/hurts?

NOTES

_____

_____

_____

_____

_____

_____

_____

_____

_____

_____

_____

_____

_____

_____

_____

_____

_____

Blob Fame: Blob idols seem to fly above mere Blobs. Have you ever wanted to be famous? Why? Would you ever consider being famous? What for?

NOTES

_____

_____

_____

_____

_____

_____

_____

_____

_____

_____

_____

_____

_____

_____

_____

_____

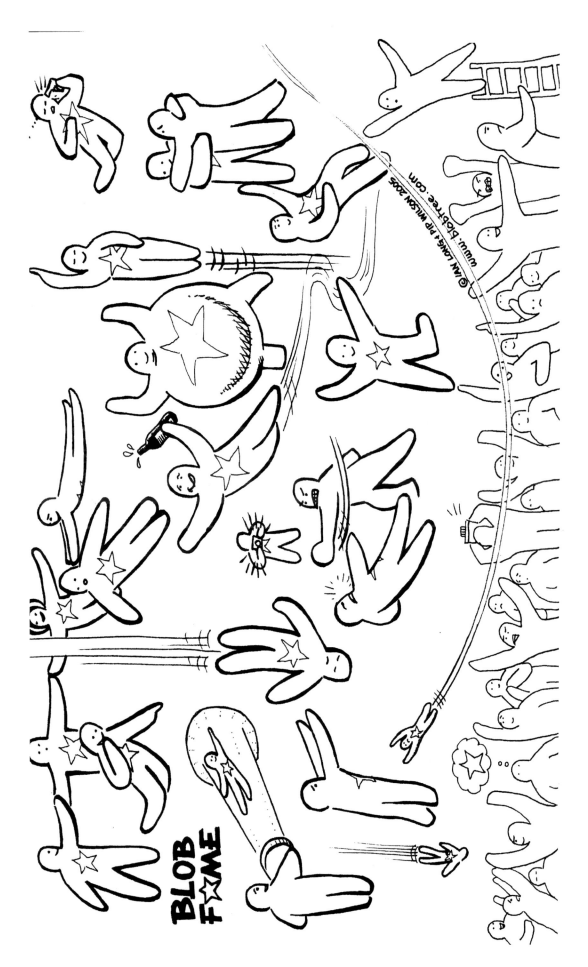

BLOB F✪ME

Blob Families: Can you find what happens in your family when arguments start? Can you order the story? Who is in charge of the family?

NOTES

_____

_____

_____

_____

_____

_____

_____

_____

_____

_____

_____

_____

_____

_____

_____

_____

BLOB FAMILIES

Blob Feast: Food is a big issue. Which table would you sit at? Why are there skinny ones? Who sits at the hungry table? Who is the chef? Where would you not sit? Why?

NOTES

_____

_____

_____

_____

_____

_____

_____

_____

_____

_____

_____

_____

_____

_____

_____

_____

57

Blob Money: If you received lots of money how would you feel? Would it change you? Which Blob do you feel like? What about your family?

NOTES

_____

_____

_____

_____

_____

_____

_____

_____

_____

_____

_____

_____

_____

_____

_____

_____

_____

Blob Parents: We are the product of our family's parenting. Which one are you. Which one disturbs you? Why do we leave our parents? Have you left?

NOTES

_____

_____

_____

_____

_____

_____

_____

_____

_____

_____

_____

_____

_____

_____

_____

_____

BLOB
PARENTS
www. blobtree.com

© IAN LONG 2004 + PIP WILSON

Blob Protests: Have you ever opposed something? It could be in your family/workplace. Which approach did you take? Will you change your approach next time?

NOTES

_____

_____

_____

_____

_____

_____

_____

_____

_____

_____

_____

_____

_____

_____

_____

_____

www.blobtree.com

BLOB PROTESTS

© IAN LONG 2004
+ PIP WILSON

Blob Romance: Can you find your love? Is there anyone you do not like? Who is about to split?

NOTES

_____

_____

_____

_____

_____

_____

_____

_____

_____

_____

_____

_____

_____

_____

_____

_____

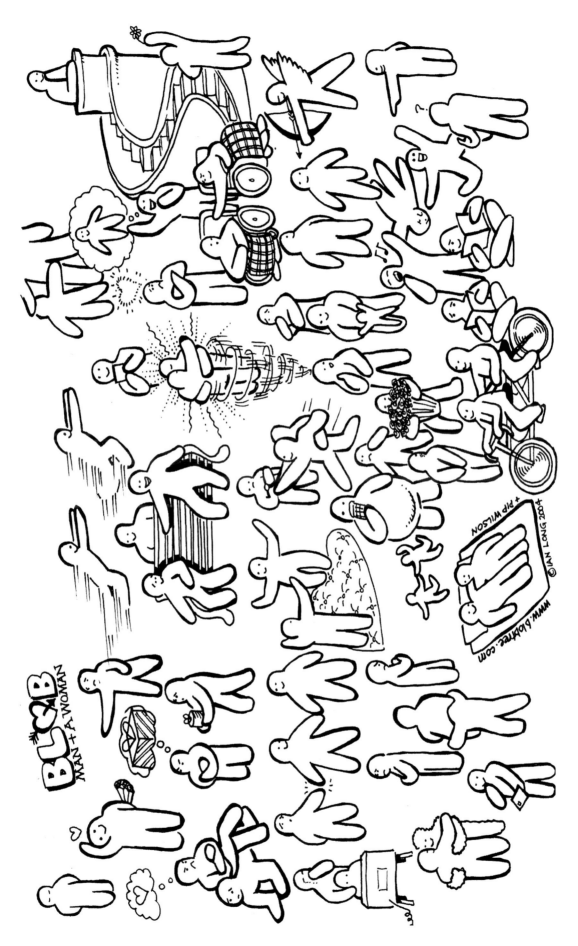

Blob Sin: Have you seen these happen? Could you ignore it? Which offends you?

NOTES

_____

_____

_____

_____

_____

_____

_____

_____

_____

_____

_____

_____

_____

_____

_____

_____

_____

Blob Sleep: Which is you? Which would you like to be? Do you sleep well at night?

NOTES

_____

_____

_____

_____

_____

_____

_____

_____

_____

_____

_____

_____

_____

_____

_____

_____

Blob Sleep: Which is you? Which would you like to be? Do you sleep well at night?

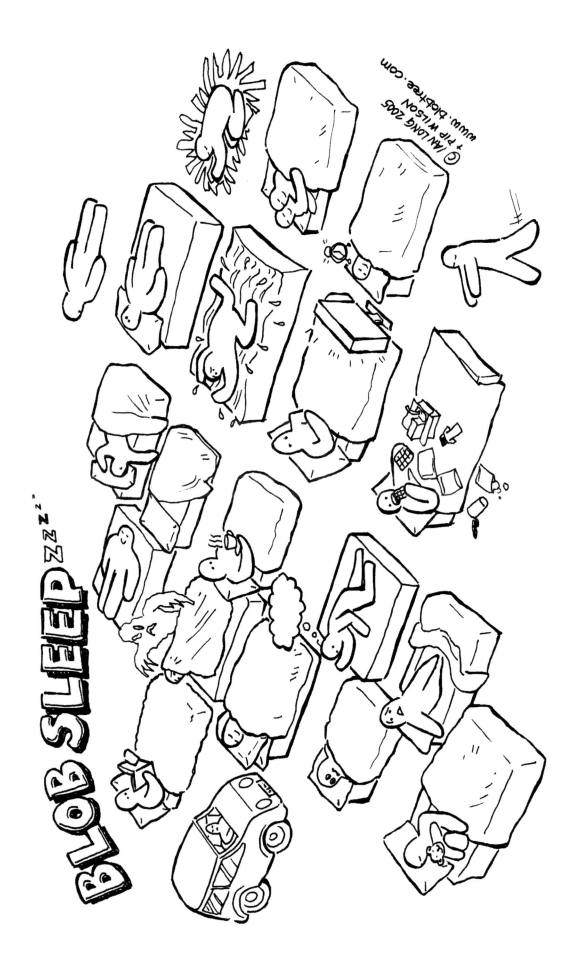

69

Blob Talk: Which method do you prefer? Can you justify using all of them?

NOTES

_____

_____

_____

_____

_____

_____

_____

_____

_____

_____

_____

_____

_____

_____

_____

_____

_____

Blob Talk: Which method do you prefer? Can you justify

www.blobtree.com

© IAN LONG 2005
+ PIP WILSON

Blob v Blob: Why do some Blobs prefer to fight? When war happens where do you stand? Would you ever kill? Why is a flag used in war?

NOTES

_____

_____

_____

_____

_____

_____

_____

_____

_____

_____

_____

_____

_____

_____

_____

_____

BLOB v BLOB

Blob Water Safety: Look at the dangers before a trip/camp. What does it symbolise?

NOTES

_____

_____

_____

_____

_____

_____

_____

_____

_____

_____

_____

_____

_____

_____

_____

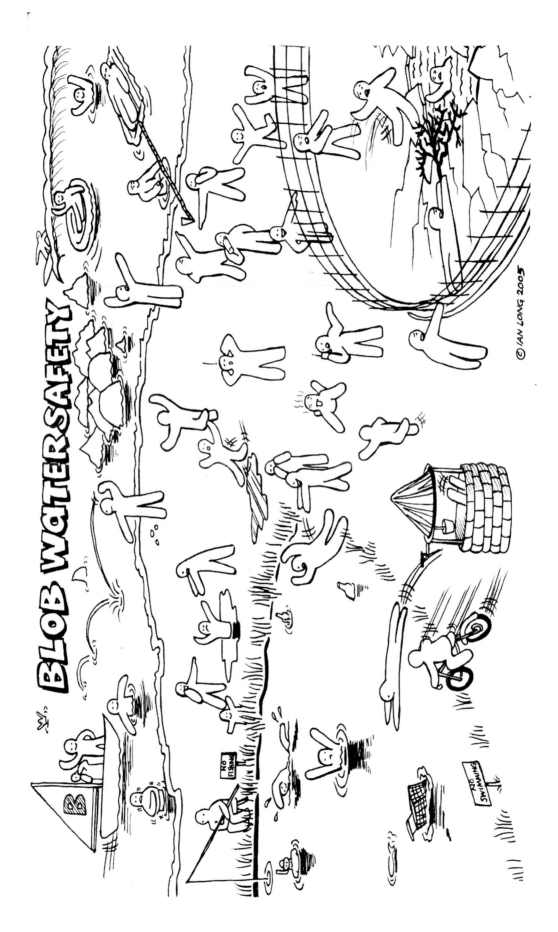

Blob World: How are we damaging the world? How can we find small ways to help? Are we helpless? Which Blob cares the most? Which is the most frustrated Blob?

NOTES

_____

_____

_____

_____

_____

_____

_____

_____

_____

_____

_____

_____

_____

_____

_____

_____

www.blobtree.com

BLOB WORLD

THEME 3: OCCASIONS

CONTENTS

Blob After 8's 83

Blob Christmas 85

Blob Easter 87

Blob Football 89

Blob Lecture 91

Blob Nativity 93

Blob Olympics 95

Sk8r Blob 97

THEME 3: OCCASIONS

This series of Blob pictures relates to special events. They can be festivals such as Christmas or weekly meetings which are significant to us. Some people make trips to the football ground while others head off to church. Why do we place importance on these occasions? Each of these images could symbolise an aspect of life. Some have been hinted at.

After-8-Blobs: Where would you sit? Who is the key Blob? Who has just joined? If you were there who would you talk to? If God was there who would he talk to? Are there any difficult situations about to happen? Would you like to be there?

NOTES

_____

_____

_____

_____

_____

_____

_____

_____

_____

_____

_____

_____

_____

_____

AFTER-8-BLOBS

www.blobtree.com

© IAN LONG 2004
+ PIP WILSON

Blob Christmas: Every year we spend months getting ready for Christmas. How do you feel? Which Blob would you like to be? Which Blobs annoy you? Which Blobs have missed the point? Which family is closest to yours? Which family is the happiest? How do you react to presents?

NOTES

_____

_____

_____

_____

_____

_____

_____

_____

_____

_____

_____

_____

_____

_____

BLOB CHRISTMAS

www.blobtree.com

Blob Easter: Do you observe the most important Christian festival? Do you celebrate it with music, chocolate or prayer? Which Blob is going too far? Which Blob needs to show more respect? Where would you stand in the crowd? Do you prefer Christmas or Easter?

NOTES

_____

_____

_____

_____

_____

_____

_____

_____

_____

_____

_____

_____

_____

_____

Blob Football: Do you like football? Which Blob would you be? If you had to play which Blob would you be? Are there any Blobs which annoy you? If the pitch symbolised life where are you – scoring goals or in the dressing rooms? How about your family? Where are you in work?

NOTES

_____

_____

_____

_____

_____

_____

_____

_____

_____

_____

_____

_____

_____

_____

Blob Lecture: The daily grind for many people. Which Blob are you in meetings? Do you look forward to being taught by others? Which group would you like to be part of? Which Blob is the leader of each table? Who is being disruptive? Why? Which table would you avoid? Would your table be different again?

NOTES

_____
_____
_____
_____
_____
_____
_____
_____
_____
_____
_____
_____
_____
_____

www.blobtree.com

91

Blob Nativity: Every year we spend months getting ready for Christmas. How do you feel? Which Blob would you like to be? Which Blobs annoy you? Which Blobs have missed the point? Which family is closest to yours? Which family is the happiest? How do you react to the Christmas story?

NOTES

_____

_____

_____

_____

_____

_____

_____

_____

_____

_____

_____

_____

_____

_____

Blob Olympics: How do you experience this four-yearly event? Are you itching to get on the track? Which Blob would you dream of being? Which Blob is the fittest? Which aspects of the Olympics annoy you? If it symbolised life rather than sport what would each Blob represent? Which Blob would you be?

NOTES

_____

_____

_____

_____

_____

_____

_____

_____

_____

_____

_____

_____

_____

_____

Sk8r Blob: Which Blob do you feel like? Which Blobs are the most skilful? Which Blobs are selling drugs? Which Blobs are supervising? Which Blobs need to go home? Which Blobs are causing trouble? Which Blob would you like to be?

NOTES

_____

_____

_____

_____

_____

_____

_____

_____

_____

_____

_____

_____

_____

_____

THEME 4: PERSONAL DEVELOPMENT

CONTENTS

Blob Balloons 103

Blob Body 105

Blob Caged 107

Blob Caring 109

Blob Doors 111

Blob Feelings 113

Blob Leaps 115

Blob River 117

Blob Rock 119

Blob Shadows 121

Level 5 Blobs 123

THEME 4: PERSONAL DEVELOPMENT

These images have the most potential for open discussion and need to be handled with care. They cover a range of feelings which could be the basis for hours of open discussion or squandered in the wrong atmosphere. As you consider whether to use one of these or not it might be worth having another image from sections 1, 2 or 3 to hand. Take the time to explore these images on your own first.

Blob Balloons: At the end of an activity you might want people to write their thoughts down in the balloons.

NOTES

_____

_____

_____

_____

_____

_____

_____

_____

_____

_____

_____

_____

_____

_____

_____

_____

_____

BLOB BALLOONS

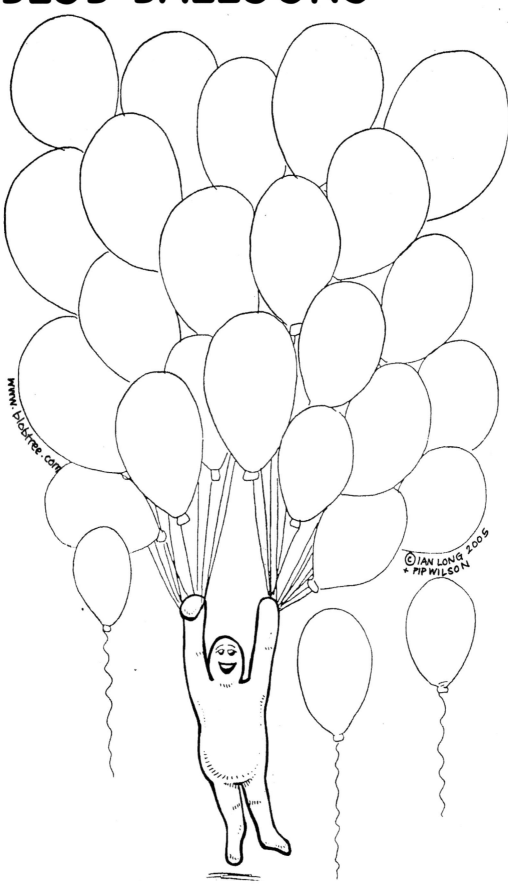

Blob Body: A powerful image of how we relate to one another is seeing your group as a body. Who is the head? Who is causing problems? Who is smashing up the unit?

NOTES

_____

_____

_____

_____

_____

_____

_____

_____

_____

_____

_____

_____

_____

_____

_____

_____

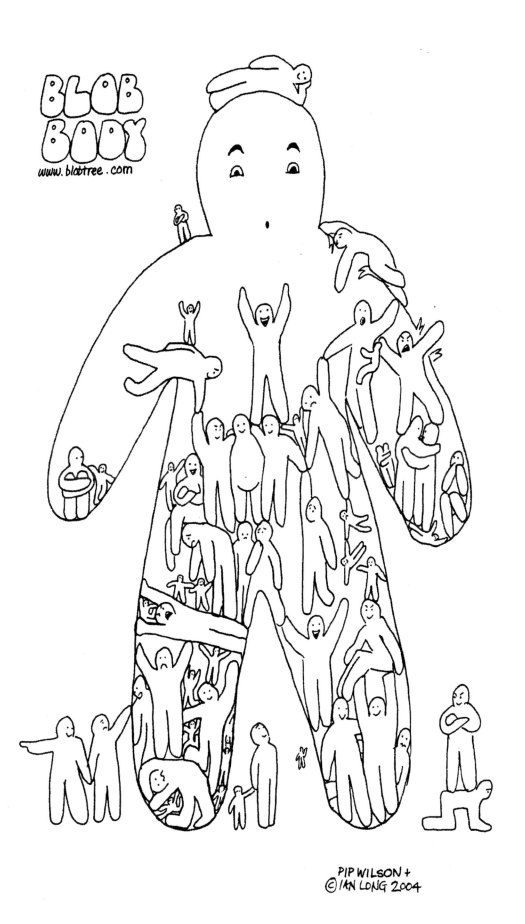

PIP WILSON +
© IAN LONG 2004

Blob Caged: A simple image with several levels to explore. What could the box symbolise? What is the timescale? Where are you in your journey?

NOTES

_____

_____

_____

_____

_____

_____

_____

_____

_____

_____

_____

_____

_____

_____

_____

_____

_____

BLOB CAGED

Blob Caring: A simple story of co-operation. When did you last experience this?

NOTES

_____

_____

_____

_____

_____

_____

_____

_____

_____

_____

_____

_____

_____

_____

_____

_____

_____

Blob Caring: A simple story of co-operation. When did you last experience this?

BLOB CARING

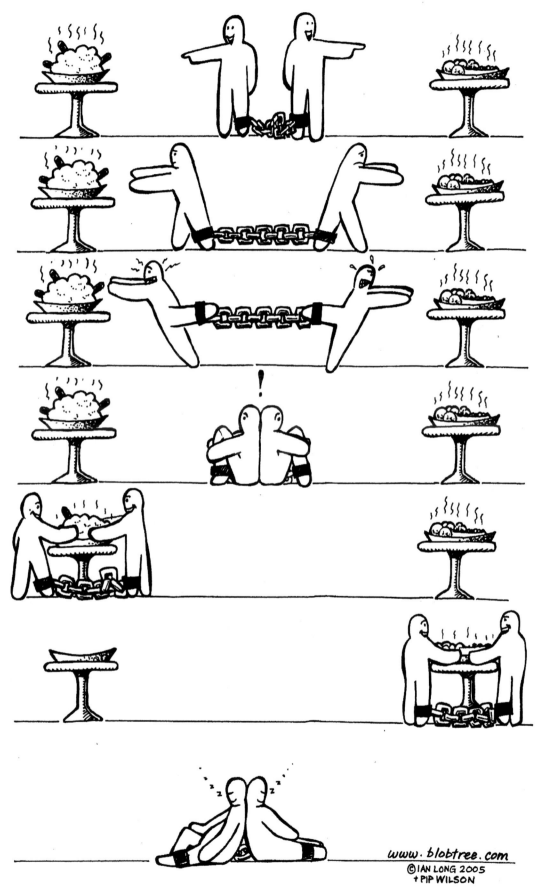

Blob Doors: Each door we pass through symbolises a new opportunity. How do you feel each time you face change? Is there any response you feel which you would like to change? What was the last door you passed through? Which door would you like to go through next?

NOTES

_____

_____

_____

_____

_____

_____

_____

_____

_____

_____

_____

_____

_____

_____

_____

BLOB DOORS

www.blobtree.com

Blob Feelings: Which Blob do you feel like now? Which Blob did you feel like this morning/last night? Which Blob would you like to be? Which Blob would you like to be friends with? Which Blob is hurting the most? Which Blob needs to pull him or herself together? Which Blob does God feel like? Which Blob will enjoy life the most?

NOTES

_____

_____

_____

_____

_____

_____

_____

_____

_____

_____

_____

_____

_____

_____

Blob feelings

©IAN LONG + PIP WILSON · www.blobtree.com

Blob Leaps: On your journey of life you have ups and downs. Which Blob would you like to be? Which Blob has an unfair advantage? Where are you so far? Why are some stuck at the start? Why do not all the Blobs at the end want to help? What has been the most terrifying part of your journey?

NOTES

_____

_____

_____

_____

_____

_____

_____

_____

_____

_____

_____

_____

_____

_____

_____

_____

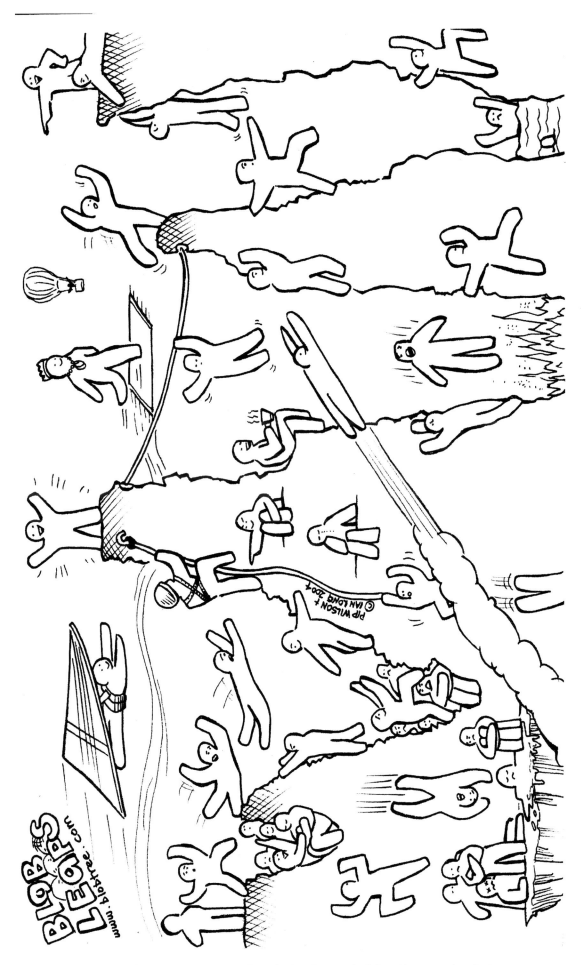

Blob River: Which Blob has experienced the river fully? Which Blob is the wisest/most foolish? If the river symbolises life where are you on the journey? What do the trees symbolise? (Based on a passage from Isaiah in the Bible.)

NOTES

_____
_____
_____
_____
_____
_____
_____
_____
_____
_____
_____
_____
_____
_____
_____

BLOB RIVER

© IAN LONG + PIP WILSON 2005

www.blobtree.com

Blob Rock: Have you ever needed rescuing? Are you a rescuer now?

NOTES

_____

_____

_____

_____

_____

_____

_____

_____

_____

_____

_____

_____

_____

_____

_____

_____

_____

Blob Shadows: Which shadow describes what lies behind you? Which were you?

NOTES

_____

_____

_____

_____

_____

_____

_____

_____

_____

_____

_____

_____

_____

_____

_____

_____

121

Level 5 Blobs: Explore the different levels. What do you notice? How could you describe each group? Which level would you like to be on? Which level are you on? Where will you be by the end of the year? Can you imagine how they all feel? What do all the activities symbolise?

NOTES

_____

_____

_____

_____

_____

_____

_____

_____

_____

_____

_____

_____

_____

_____

The Blobs Training Manual

An encompassing manual to explain the full use of all the Blob resources

By Pip Wilson & Ian Long

Eagerly awaited, this comprehensive resource book for understanding and using the Blobs provides:

• A fantastic insight into Blobs and Blob Trees, their development and the theory behind them
• Clear instructions on how Blobs can be used to discuss a wide variety of important issues emotions and feelings • Session ideas and activities for working with groups and individuals of all ages
• Questions to use with the Blobs • What not to do when using Blobs.

This manual is ideal for anyone new to the Blobs resources and will also provide background information and additional ideas for those familiar with this engaging series.

All ages   *116 pages*   **Ref 002-5672**

Feelings Blob Cards

Initiate discussion and reflection about feelings

People of all ages can relate to these appealing Blob characters – even young children can recognise when they start to feel like these 'funny people'. So, to get people talking about feelings, turn up a card and see which blob you get. They may be angry, happy, depressed or excited – the cards span a whole range of emotions.

The accompanying booklet contains loads of suggestions for activities: with small or large groups, and one to one.

All ages   *48 full-colour cards 125 x 80mm, boxed*   **Ref 003-5482**

Emotions Blob Cards

Encourage children to talk about emotions

The groups of Blobs on these cards are acting in many familiar 'human' ways: celebrating, fighting, feeling left out, supporting or ignoring each other. Looking at Blobs together instead of alone enables you to explore a wide range of feelings and emotions to do with personal and social interaction. Includes a booklet with lots of ideas for activities.

All ages   *48 full-colour cards 125 x 80mm, boxed*

Ref 003-5483

Family Blob Cards

48 Blob cards to promote discussion and reflection on the family

By Pip Wilson & Ian Long

The various family scenarios depicted in this card set provide an opportunity for individuals or groups to discuss all aspects of family life and the situations that arise from it.

• Each scenario is colour coded with 6-9 cards telling a short story
• The cards can also be used individually, or combined to create other situations
• Includes more than 50 suggestions for use on the accompanying activity cards.

All ages   *48 full-colour cards, 125 x 80mm + 8 instruction cards, boxed*   **Ref 003-5621**

Teenage Life Blob Cards

An effective tool to explore teenage issues

By Pip Wilson & Ian Long

Blobs are a way of communicating using two of the first languages learnt as children – body language and feelings. These cards provide a tool to consider and discuss a multitude of positive and negative teenager feelings and behaviours. They can be used individually or for group work and cover topics such as:

• Relationships and friendships • Bullying • Addiction • Emotions• Confidence • Self-image.

All ages   *48 full-colour 125 x 80mm boxed cards, suggesting over 50 optional activities.*

Ref 003-5664

VALUE! BUY ALL 4 SETS AT A SAVING
BLOB CARDS SET OF 4   **Ref 003-5689**

Other Blob Resources

By Pip Wilson and Ian Long

❯❯ Blob Tree Posters

Four unique posters to help children talk about feelings

By Pip Wilson & Ian Long

These blob tree posters can be used by whole classes, small groups or on a one-to-one basis to initiate and promote discussion of feelings. The internationally renowned 'blob' figures are non-threatening and appeal to all ages. Each poster contains a different set of feelings to explore and discuss. Includes notes for guidance.

All ages *4 encapsulated posters. Size 30.5 x 42.5cm*

Ref 003-5485

best seller

" Wow - I love them - innovative, practical, creative and enabling. These posters are going to be very useful to all schools looking for ways to facilitate and develop the pupil voice."
Carol Smart, SNIP

❯❯ Mini Blob Tree Posters

BY POPULAR DEMAND! These mini blob tree posters can be used for individual or group work

All ages *16 x A5 posters (4 of each)*

Ref 003-5486

A5 SIZE

VALUE! BUY BOTH AT A SAVING   BLOB TREE & MINI BLOB TREE POSTERS   Ref 003-5487

Other Blob Resources

By Pip Wilson and Ian Long

›› Blob Posters

Four posters to help children talk about specific emotions

By Pip Wilson & Ian Long

From the creators of the hugely successful blob tree phenomenon - four more posters on the specific emotions of: • Happy • Disappointed • Calm • Anger

Includes notes for guidance

All ages *4 encapsulated posters. Size 30.5 x 42.5cm*

Ref 003-5520

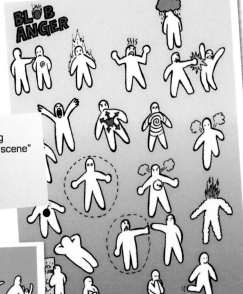

"Everyone sees something personal to them in each scene"
Jean Ruggin, College Controller, Beacon Community College, East Sussex

›› Mini Blob Posters

BY POPULAR DEMAND! These mini blob posters can be used for individual or group work

All ages *16 x A5 posters (4 of each)*

Ref 003-5515

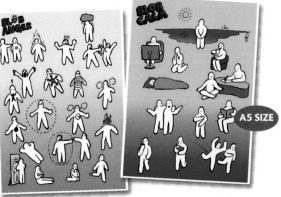

A5 SIZE

best seller

⏫ Giant Blob Feelings Poster

Over 50 individual blobs on one giant poster!

By Pip Wilson & Ian Long

With so many blob pictures on one poster you will never run out of ideas for discussion. Includes notes for guidance.

`All ages` *Size: A1 [84 x 59.4cm] laminated*

Ref 003-5518

"This poster attracts attention from everyone. People come into my office to look at how they are feeling today! A great starting point!"
Ms Sharon Cohen, Learning Mentor at Eglinton Primary School & EYC

"Perfect at helping children to express what they think they are feeling"
J Karen Barwick, Learning Mentor at Millhouse Junior School

 A1 SIZE

VALUE! PURCHASE 4 POSTERS AT A SAVING GIANT BLOB FEELINGS POSTER SET Ref 003-5651

⏩ The Big Book of Blob Trees

50 different blob trees to explore feelings

By Pip Wilson & Ian Long

This unique collection of blob trees with all its various Blob characters is a fabulous way of opening up discussions about feelings and developing the understanding of emotions, empathy and self-awareness. The different trees show various scenarios that individuals or groups may experience personally.

The book comes with guidance and suggested questions such as:

- Which Blob do you feel like?
- Find a Blob that interests you?
- Which Blob confuses you?
- Which Blob annoys you the most? Why?

The Blobs can also be used in less personal ways so you ask which Blob is happy, why do you think he is happy and discussion can evolve that way indirectly. This resource can be used with individuals or groups.

best seller

`All ages` *125 pages, A4*
Ref 002-5617

⏪ Blobtastic Sticker Book

1,800 colourful reward stickers

The *Blobtastic Sticker Book* is made up of six different designs of blob characters. Each blob character is depicted with star quality so makes the perfect reward and motivational aid for children.

`All ages` *1,800 coloured stickers in 6 different designs, A4*
Ref 002-5619

⏩ Blob Feelings Ball

An animated way to discuss feelings

By Pip Wilson & Ian Long

Throw, roll, pass the ball and the recipient then chooses a Blob character that best describes how they feel. The ball illustrates a variety of Blob characters which depict various feelings such as:

- Happiness • Sadness • Anger • Wary • Fear.

The ball comes with guidance giving suggestions for use, including ideas for questions.

`All ages` *Approx size: 20cm*
Ref 003-5620

Other Blob Resources

By Pip Wilson and Ian Long

» The Blob Collection

Collection of 15 Blob products

Blob Feelings Ball, The Big Book of Blob Trees, Blobtastic Sticker Book, Feelings Blob Cards, Emotions Blob Cards, Blob Tree Posters, Mini Blob Tree Posters, Big Book of Blobs, Big Book of Blob Feelings, Blob Posters, Mini Blob Posters, Giant Blob Feelings Poster, Teenage Life Blob Cards, Family Blob Cards, The Blob Training Manual.

All ages   Ref 003-5629